Emerging *from* the Mess

Finding Hope in Life's Storms

Brendan McManus SJ
& Jim Deeds

Published by Messenger Publications, 2024

Copyright © Brendan McManus SJ and Jim Deeds, 2024

The right of Brendan McManus SJ and Jim Deeds to be identified as the authors of the Work has been asserted by them in accordance with the Copyright and Related Rights Act, 2000. All rights reserved. No part of this book may be reproduced or utilised in any form or by any means electronic or mechanical including photography, filming, recording, video recording, photocopying or by any information storage and retrieval system or shall not by way of trade or otherwise be lent, resold or otherwise circulated in any form of binding or cover other than that in which it is published without prior permission in writing from the publisher.

Scripture quotations are taken from the New Revised Standard Version Updated Edition. Copyright © 2021 National Council of Churches of Christ in the United States of America. Used by permission. All rights reserved worldwide.

ISBN: 9781788126601

Designed by Brendan McCarthy
Typeset in Palatino Regular and The Seasons
Printed by Hussar Books

Messenger Publications,
37 Lower Leeson Street, Dublin 2
www.messenger.ie

Contents

Introduction 9

1: On the Rocks 14
An involuntary retreat 17
Going to the dark, empty places 21
Asking for mercy 23
For those who grieve 27
Dealing with mistakes 30
The beauty of broken things 33
Dealing with bad news 35

2: Lost at Sea
Believing that we are forgiven 40
What you really want or desire 43
Prayers for commendation 47
It's not about the money 49
Looking deeper: seeing the
'process' behind the 'product' 53
Stripping back 57

Contents

3: Sailing Home

The importance of saying 'Yes' 63

A deeper brush 65

Not walking on by 68

Praying for a thaw 71

Small steps on the spiritual journey home 74

Getting a tune up 77

4: Arriving in Port

A plan greater than our own 82

Praying with your body 85

Praying for peace 89

Being thankful 92

Your heart is where your treasure is 95

Stopping to smell the roses 98

Conclusion: 102

Introduction

In our journey of finding God in the mess over the last seven years we have been blessed with all the people we've come into contact with, whether through retreats, meetings or online. Using scripture in particular, we discovered that it helped people to pray and to bring their particular situation or 'mess' to God. Particularly in the aftermath of the Covid-19 pandemic, which saw the loss of so many things – freedom, relationships and autonomy – we wanted to write something on hope or 'emerging from the mess'. Just like the grief process itself, there is a dying and then a rising. Like a self-righting buoy, something always brings us back to the light. At the darkest hour the dawn arrives again anew, just like always, but we forget so easily. The image of the lighthouse also captures this reality of the light that brings us through the storms to a safe port. This world of uncertainty, drought, war and death is not the end. It's not all of reality as it proposes to be but just a temporary place of growth and purification. We are unexpectedly redeemed, saved from the grave. We learn about humility, compassion and grace. A person, the Christ, has lifted us up. Our true destiny is revealed to be with the Light, breaking open the clouds of a weary, often isolated existence.

This experience is at the heart of the Spiritual Exercises, the classic Ignatian retreat process based on the experience of St Ignatius Loyola. The first week begins with the joy and wonder of God's grace, then the coming of Christ, the light; but very soon we hit the wall in the third week with the pain of the Passion of Christ and all seems lost. The wisdom of the retreat is such that we have to arrive at these very dark places of disintegration and loss to appreciate the resurrection; it is God's world, and in God's time things swing around. The death–resurrection experience is a process of slowly coming back to life and recovering the joy of simply being again. The key to it is being grateful for small things. Being in the passion, the trough, or the dip though robs us of the 'feel-good' factor, of the simple pleasures of good sleep, inner peace and being on top of things. The danger is losing perspective and motivation. We have to trust the process. It is only by reaching our limits that we break through them.

The life and death of Jesus is not something that happened years ago and is no longer relevant, rather it is the very essence of the lives we live. The dying and the rising is a continual process that marks our lives and especially shapes our post-pandemic world. Emerging from the mess is essentially the experience of how suffering and pain alternates with great joy and fulfilment. Especially when we reach the limits of our strength and endurance (Richard Rohr calls this 'liminal space'), we need to remember to hang on, to be patient and faithful in prayer. This is the very experience that Jesus himself passed through in the Garden of Gethsemane, the 'why have you forsaken me' moment (Mt 27:46) that is chilling but inspiring in its raw humanity. It invites us to make this same radical prayer, the prayer of the cross, imitating the same U-shaped process that Jesus has lived through. Reaching the limits and handing it all over to God, holding nothing back, stepping into that dangerous mysterious void.

Then, before we know it, hope awakens, and we can see the spring outside. We hear the birds again, carried and inspired, the world seems all right, the pain drifts away. The hardest thing is hanging on in the bottom of the dive and remembering that it's not about us, that we are being carried and need to let ourselves be lifted and freed. The challenge is to live every day like a resurrection day. It is all about gratitude: to see the absolute giftedness of every moment, the wonder of every encounter, the silver lining on every cloud. We have structured this book in four sections to mirror this exact same process of desolation to hope, darkness to light, and the eleventh hour rescue from despair.

Praying (your way) out of the Mess
Using the structure of the Ignatian Examen and the Spiritual Exercises, and especially the structure of a typical prayer session, this book allows the reader to build their own individually customised prayer by selecting from the following, adapting as needed.

Prepare yourself
Clear a space, use music or breathing to focus, do a body scan, how am I physically, emotionally and spiritually?

Make a prayer of connection
Offer yourself to God from wherever you find yourself.

Ask for a grace
Ask for what you want sure directly, bring your 'mess' to mind, name what you want from God, formulate it as a grace, a gift from God.

Choose a story
We have provided a wide variety of texts to cover many different human experiences and provided you with a question and piece of scripture for contemplation.

Reflect
Look back over what you have read and prayed with. What was God saying to you?

Act
Commit yourself to some action, ask for advice, mend a relationship, change your habits, act against negative influences, do more prayer etc.

Closing prayer
Give thanks for what you have received, ask forgiveness for mistakes, hand it all over to God, pray for others (petition).

Brendan & Jim

1
On the Rocks

An involuntary retreat

An involuntary retreat

The time of lockdown was like an involuntary retreat. I had to spend a lot of time with myself, even while looking after my mother. Having done a lot of spiritual retreats over the years, I sort of knew what to expect and how to survive this difficult time. It was further complicated in that my mother was becoming more unwell, and I was under more pressure as a care giver.

Initially there was a honeymoon period, the initial naïve joy about having a lot of time, reduced commitments and time to unwind. Then, however, came the disillusionment: with so much time and being isolated with others, I had to face myself. In some ways my normal life of activity, busyness, and distractions allowed me to coast along on the surface and avoid any deeper issues. In isolation there was no choice but to be with myself, and this was tough, as a lot of unpleasant feelings, memories and issues came to the surface.

At this point I knew I had a choice. I could do what many did: react against the process and strive to distract and entertain myself. That's one strategy. Another was to find a way through, to befriend myself and be reconciled. This probably sounds a bit odd. Surely I know myself and have nothing to learn through this?

The crunch was that I needed a sense of the divine – of the transcendent or of God – to be able to make this crucial transition. All spiritual paths speak of this experience of a dark night, 'purgatory' (purifying), the Cross or passion. Essentially it was a sense of being carried or held by compassionate love that was needed to understand my identity (as a creature), my need of healing, and finding a path forward, especially in being with my mum at this crucial time.

Some blocks that I hit during this time alone were: traumatic memories, negative thoughts, a negative image of God, strong emotions that threatened to overwhelm, and a lack of self-esteem. Again it was understandable that these would arise in this lockdown context; it was like a time of purification. I was, however, able to deal with them well, through the help of prayer, a spiritual director, and a counsellor, even though it was done online. Now that she has passed, that time I had looking after my mother is a precious memory.

If we approach our times of isolation or 'involuntary retreat' in this way, we can come to love ourselves, heal memories and wounds, accept all our broken parts, and be at peace with the past. Often a meditation on acceptance and healing is needed to explicitly acknowledge our relationship to the divine and our desperate need for love. It is liberating.

Prayer
God, help me to remember that you are with me always, even in dark times when you feel absent and remote. Keep me faithful to prayer and let me always believe that you are a merciful, forgiving God who always gives me a way back home. Amen.

Scripture
Out of the depths I cry to you, Lord;
Lord, hear my voice.
Let your ears be attentive
to my cry for mercy. (Psalm 130:1–2)

Going to the dark empty places

We all have experience of darkness in life at times. The darkness comes in those places where our shadows trip us up. For some those shadows are shadows of anger or unforgiveness or ill-health. For others broken relationships or financial worries might be the shadows that dwell in the dark, empty places.

I am no different, of course. I have my own dark and empty places, where shadows terrify me. My own shadow is anxiety. A recent spiritual direction session helped me to come to an insight; at the first sign of anxiety beginning to mess with me, I often try to outrun it. I throw myself into work, or I avoid quietness and reflection in case I encounter my anxiety and well, I'm not quite sure what I fear will happen in that place. Indeed the paradox is that the very thing that I avoid is what is needed to get a hold on my shadows.

It is in facing into the dark and empty place that we can see the reality that our problems, though sometimes seemingly great in size or magnitude, are never the entirety of the story. For me slowing down and regaining the discipline of prayer and reflection rather than bringing me to a place of terror and ruin actually takes me to a place of healing. It's a place of encounter with reality, of encounter with God.

On Holy Saturday each year, silence falls, and the

dark and empty tomb screams out to those who would fear the end, 'Come, see!' And I see now why they had to go to the tomb. Jesus was teaching them, even in a time of great misery, that we all have to go to the tomb – the dark and empty places – scary and all as that may be. Why does he call us there? Because when we go, when we face into the darkness, we will see that it is not dark at all. A wonderful light is coming. Problems, even death, are not the end. There is always the promise of three days later.

Prayer
God, sometimes it is hard to face into worries and problems. It is easier to run away or to avoid them. Help us to go to the dark and empty places, knowing that when we do, we will find there your wonderful light of healing. Amen.

Scripture
Hear my prayer, O Lord,
and give ear to my cry;
do not hold your peace at my tears. (Psalm 39:12)

Asking for mercy

Asking for mercy

It is the end of the road. The days are dark, the nights more so. All seems lost. Our hearts are heavy. What can we cry? Surely the only thing left in these circumstances is to cry, 'I am done! I cannot do this! I need … something!' Have you been there? Are you maybe there right now? 'Lord have mercy' is the cry of someone with nothing left.

Yet it is really the cry of someone who has everything they need to dream of something better. How so? The only valid way to approach God is with the humility of knowing we are not enough on our own. We cannot approach God in any other way. For is it we who need God or God who needs us? Approaching God with a sense of it's okay God, I've got most of this, and I only need you for you these very specific requests, is not real surrender to God at all. When we cry out 'Lord, have mercy', we do so in complete surrender. We know, in those moments, that we cannot do it, anything, on our own.

The surrender of the cry 'Lord, have mercy' is heard again and again in scripture. We think of blind Bartimaeus by the side of the road: poor, hungry, ignored, outcast. He cries out as he sees Jesus, 'Son of David, have mercy on me!' (Luke 18:38). We think of the younger son in the parable of the Prodigal Son or the Forgiving Father, who comes begging to his father for mercy. We think of the woman about to be stoned by judgemental men who fell at Jesus' feet in the moments before she was to be stoned to death.

We don't have to go as far as our scriptural

tradition, do we? We know, ourselves, what it is to cry out in complete surrender, in knowing we cannot do it by ourselves. Many don't have the language of the Church or of God, even, but we know what it is to cry out. We cry out in surrender in the face of the economic crisis that could see our brothers and sisters freezing and starving this winter as the rich get richer. We know what it is to be helpless in the face of nuclear threats from tyrants. We know what it is to grieve and miss our loved ones and wonder whether we will see them again. We know as much as any bible character from long ago. We know.

And yet, they teach us a lesson, echoing down through the years. Let's look at the few examples that I gave. Bartimaeus calls for mercy and is healed. The younger son in the parable calls for mercy and is welcomed back into his family. The woman wrongly judged calls for mercy and goes free, loved by God. Calls for mercy, surrender to God, acknowledgement that we cannot do this by ourselves, all are met by the love of God.

Prayer
God, let us be humble enough to make real prayers out of our need and helplessness. Let us be vessels of your mercy to those we meet. Let us be open to be challenged by the need for mercy in our world right now. Let us be open to hear the cries of others in distress and be able to respond with mercy and compassion. Amen.

Scripture
When he heard that it was Jesus of Nazareth, he began to shout, 'Jesus, Son of David, have mercy on me!' (Mark 10:47)

For those who grieve

I remember the first person I knew that died. She was a friend of my grandfather, and we had visited her together many times on the walks he took me on as a child. I was about ten when she died. She was the first person I saw in a coffin, and it was the first time that I was so obviously confronted with the fact that life here on earth was not infinite. Perhaps you remember your first experience too.

As life has gone on, of course, I have had lots more experiences of people dying. Many of these experiences involved losing someone close to me – family members and friends. No one goes through life without losing someone close.

Life leads, inevitably, to death; just like the liturgical year brings us to Lent and leads inevitably to the cross and to the death of Jesus. However just as the story of Jesus is not over on Good Friday with his death, so too our story is not over with our own death. Jesus came to teach us many things: he taught us how to live well, he taught us how to accept the finite nature of our lives, and he taught us that this life is but a staging post on the journey towards eternal life.

That said, and even accepted, losing someone close is a painful experience. The pain we feel is a measure of the love we share with our lost one. Today let us unite ourselves with those who are grieving.

For those who grieve

If you are grieving, please know that there are people united with you in your grief.

Prayer
God, help us to live well while we still possess the gift of life you have given us. Help us to accept our lives as finite. Strengthen us in our belief that through death we walk through the door of eternal life. Comfort those who are grieving right now. Help them to know that you are holding their loved one in your arms of infinite goodness, and that we will all be reunited one day. Amen.

Scripture
He said, 'Where have you laid him?' They said to him, 'Lord, come and see.' Jesus wept. Then said the Jews, 'See how much he loved him!' (John 11:34–36)

Dealing with mistakes

Dealing with mistakes

Most days, if not every day, I get to a point in the day when I can pat myself on the back and declare that I have not made a single mistake. I can be smug because I have not hurt anyone, thought bad thoughts, been selfish or grumpy. At that point of the day – and yes, I get to this point every day (how wonderful I am!) – I can say that I have pretty much done all that could have been asked of me. At that point of the day ... I switch the morning alarm off, pull back the bed covers and get up to start my day!

Each day is filled with moments of falling from grace – of making mistakes, of failing, of missing the mark. For most of us, most of the time, these moments are almost inevitable. It is our imperfections that mean we are in need of something bigger than ourselves in order to grow. Christians will call that something 'salvation' or 'redemption'.

I am not advocating purposely messing things up or not caring about yourself, others or God. It's just that if we get stuck in self-punishing mode in the face of our imperfections, we will never be happy, and we will never grow.

There are lots of examples of where Jesus, when faced with the imperfections of those around him, showed mercy and compassion and willed that the person learned from their mistakes and grew into a better way of being. In other and more modern words, he cut them a break and looked kindly on them.

Perhaps we could adopt a similar approach with ourselves and others around us? In the face of being cut a break and looked on kindly (as opposed to being shut out, judged or condemned), we are more likely to feel strong enough to give our all to growing into a better way of being. And this effort at giving our all, our best effort, no matter how small that best effort might seem, is what pleases God. We see this in the Gospel of Mark where Jesus recognises and, indeed, honours the 'widow's mite', the small amount she gave that was at the same time giving all she could.

No day is perfect. No person is perfect. Mistakes and failures are part of the journey. We grow and learn much more in the face of being cut a break and looked on kindly than judgement and being shut out.

Prayer
God, we make mistakes, and we are sorry for this. Look on us kindly in your mercy, that we may grow from our mistakes and grow into better ways of being. Help us to cut ourselves a break when we mess up, seeking to be kind to ourselves and learn from our mistakes. Help us to adopt this stance towards others who make mistakes, particularly those who have hurt us in the process. Amen.

Scripture
Then he called his disciples and said to them, 'Truly I tell you, this poor widow has put in more than all those who are contributing to the treasury. For all of them have contributed out of their abundance, but she out of her poverty has put in everything she had, all she had to live on.' (Mark 12:43–44)

The beauty of broken things

Sometimes, I feel broken, like I just don't work like I used to, want to, or need to. I guess everyone gets to feeling like this from time to time … A while ago, a very kind and wise friend called me to his garage to show me something that he thought I might be interested in. We walked together down his flowery garden path and pushed our way into a typically cluttered garage space. He dug around in lots of cardboard boxes, sifting through ornaments, photographs and goodness knows what, before coming back to me with an arm full of dark coloured wood.

'I couldn't bear to throw it out', he said, and I realised that although 'it' was in two pieces, 'it' was one 'it' rather than two. He went on to explain that at one time these two pieces had indeed been one and they made a piece of bog-oak art. When held together, they resembled a bird in that very vague and mystical way that bog-oak art does. He had bought the piece some twenty-seven years before and placed it on show in his house but it had fallen and was broken, seemingly beyond repair. However he thought that I might like to have it and use it for carving other pieces. I'm so glad he did!

The wood itself was 3,000-year-old bog oak from County Tipperary. It is dark and textured and looks as old as it is. I relished the thought of working with something so wonderful and transforming what was

The beauty of broken things

once beautiful as one thing into something beautiful as another thing or rather things, plural, because I've made many pieces out of it.

The brokenness was not the end for that piece of art. And brokenness for us (pieces of art, all that we are) is not the end of the story either. Many of us experience feelings of brokenness, exile from our normality, alienation from friends, family, ourselves even. When this happens, the temptation is to throw in the towel, to feel like giving up. But let us consider this piece of ancient bog oak and the ancient wisdom it teaches us: this too shall pass; this is not the end; things will get better.

Prayer
We pray that we will be able to dust ourselves off and transform ourselves with God's help. We ask to encounter other people in our lives who will help with this transformation. And, above all, that God would look on us as works of art and will us to be transformed. Amen.

Scripture
For we are what he has made us, created in Christ Jesus for good works, which God prepared beforehand so that we may walk in them. (Ephesians 2:10)

Dealing with bad news

Dealing with bad news

I was walking my dogs around my district one evening, when I saw a woman ahead of me. She looked agitated and angry. She began to shout loudly at a man standing directly across the road from her. She shouted, 'Are you serious?' She repeated herself a few times. The man stared at her intently with a frown on his face but said nothing. He began to cross the road to her. I slowed my pace, anticipating a confrontation – would I need to step in?

As he came close to her, he said something that I could not hear. Her response was to fall into his arms and begin to weep. He held her tightly and not a word passed between them. I walked on, casting a glance back to them for a couple of minutes as I went further down the road. They simply held each other in the middle of the footpath. Eventually they walked off, arms wrapped tightly around each other.

My sense of what happened is that the man was delivering bad news to the woman. What I had interpreted in her as agitation and anger had in fact been shock and disbelief, I think. His intent stare and silence across the road belied the fact that the message he was to deliver had to be delivered quietly and up close. Whatever the nature of the message he gave her, it stopped her in her tracks and left her distressed. I feel in my spirit that it may have been news of death or illness.

Receiving bad news is something many of us have

gone through and all of us will go through at some point. We may find ourselves shocked and distressed like the woman I saw that evening. This is a natural reaction. I was struck by the quiet, dignified and caring actions of the man that evening. He cared for this woman (and she for him), and he held her in her distress. What a gift he was to her in that moment.

Prayer
God, we pray for those who are receiving bad news today. Their shock, distress and pain may be considerable. May they have quiet, caring people around them to hold them tightly. May the bereaved know comfort. May the sick know healing. May we all know the embrace of a loving God and hold those in distress in our prayers and our loving action. Amen.

Scripture
In my distress I called upon the Lord;
to my God I called.
From his temple he heard my voice,
and my cry came to his ears. (2 Samuel 22:7)

2
Lost at Sea.

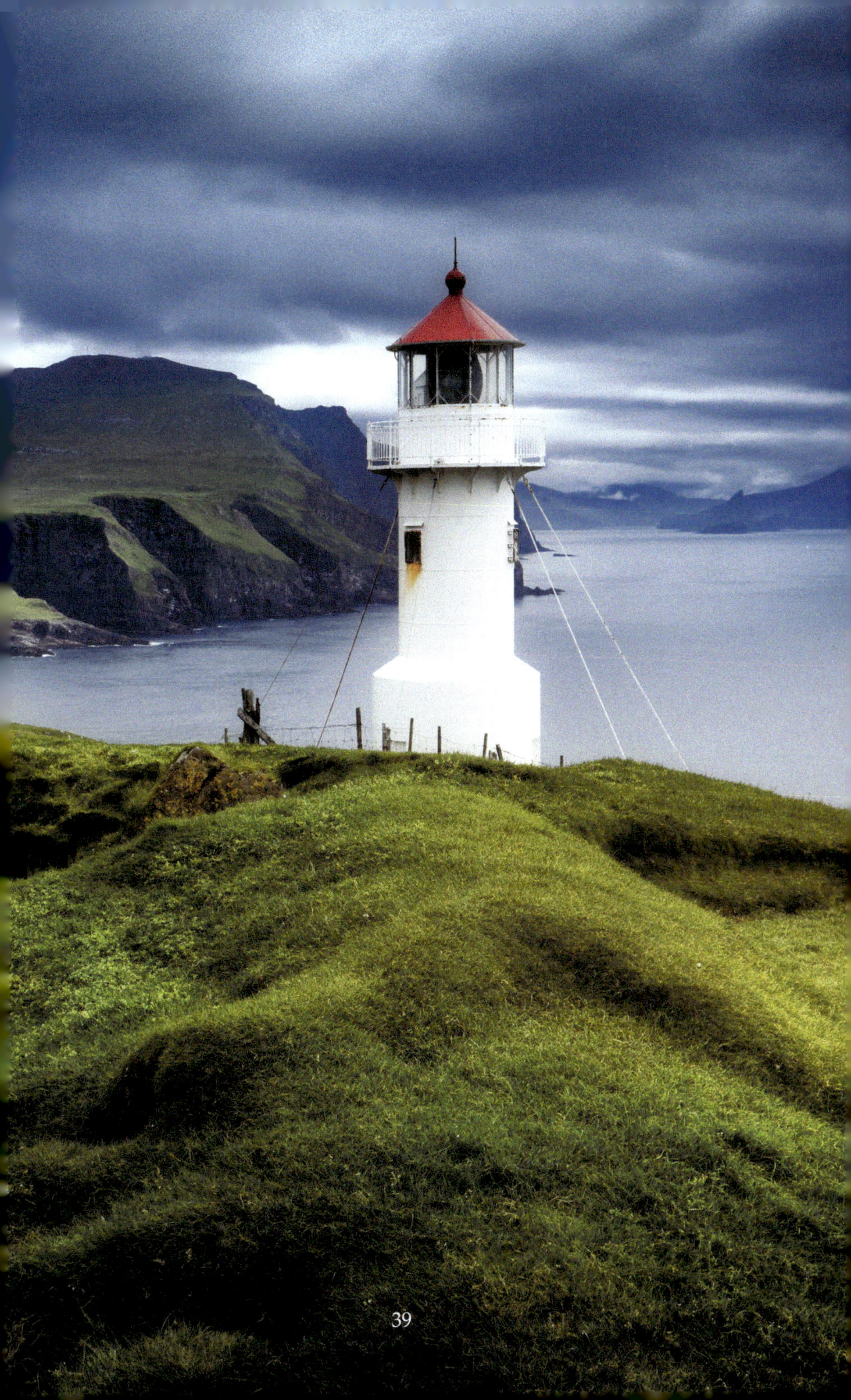

40

Believing that we are forgiven

We all have had the experience at one time or another of messing things up totally and wondering if we will be forgiven. The story of the prodigal son, which applies as much to daughters as sons, is an extraordinary story of mistakes and forgiveness.

Firstly we have the son from the title of the story – the prodigal. 'Prodigal' is a word that comes from the Latin for lavish. In this case it refers to the lavish and wasteful lifestyle this son lives after persuading his father to cut him loose from his tasks on the farm, give him his share of his inheritance and let him go his merry way. He could have stopped him, although knowing headstrong and hedonistic young men as I do – having been one – I would say that the father was wise to allow him to go his own way. The son proceeds to eat, drink and cavort his way through his money and ends up in terrible trouble, starving and lonely. What do we learn from him so far? We too can be impatient. We can be driven by desires and money and consumption. When we reflect on life, we can see that responding to these desires impatiently never has a happy end.

Having ended up starved and alone, the son, in desperation and in recognition of the goodness of his father, comes back home. He plans to work as one of the hired hands on his father's farm. Sometimes a crisis or a bit of heartache leads us to our senses it seems. And so, he goes to face the second character for us to consider here, his father.

The real focal point of the story comes in the moment of the father welcoming the son back with pure forgiveness. The father was not caught unawares by the return of the son. He was searching for him on the horizon. And even before the son had fully returned, the father had run to meet him. The image of a father who 'fell' on his son's neck evokes such emotion. We can see that it would have been a reconnecting of the two amid tears and embraces. The son may have hidden his face and claimed unworthiness. He may have cried with regret and shame at the hurt he caused. The father may have listened and loved.

Prayer
God, we believe you are full of mercy, compassion and forgiveness. Let us believe that we have a God who waits and watches for us, who runs to meet us and who falls upon our necks with hugs, kisses and tears of love. Let us believe that we can be forgiven and restored to our former dignity no matter what. Amen.

Scripture
He [the Prodigal Son] arose and came to his father. But while he was still far off, his father saw him, and was moved with compassion, and ran towards him, and fell on his neck, and kissed him. (Luke 15:11–32, KJV))

What you really want or desire

What you really want or desire

When life is tough and things seem dark, it can often help to focus on what you really want. It is a way of keeping hope alive and also getting in touch with what God wants for us. It can help to ask these questions: What is my dream? My deepest desire? Have I given myself the gift of spending time considering this?

We have lots of wants; we always want things that we think will make us happy, but these are often not our deepest desires. My deepest desires are not about wants. Wants often come from 'the surface' and can be superficial. They usually involve 'things'. The more important question is about our deepest desires, our dreams, what will bring us true happiness. They come from a place way below the surface or the superficial things. They come from a place we sometimes don't even really understand.

Ignatius said that we can find God in our deepest desires. That's a remarkable statement if we carry it through to practice. Spending time dreaming about our deepest desires might just bring us into a sacred space.

Here's another remarkable thought. A very wise friend said some time ago that if we say 'Yes' to God, God will make that 'Yes' happen, even if what we are saying 'Yes' to is something we hadn't planned for in life or something that we don't feel capable of doing.

In other words, our 'Yes' from a position of faith is fertile ground for God to be at God's work. Think of Mary's 'Yes' to the angel that brought about Jesus' coming into the world.

None of this has anything to do with us; it has nothing to do with us getting things. It's way more profound and way more meaningful for our lives and the lives of those around us. We might even not see ourselves 'gaining' anything at all in a worldly sense. We simply align ourselves with God. We dream God's dream.

Putting this together, if we dream God's dream for our lives, find our deepest desires, way beyond surface wants, and say 'Yes' to God, we can see God's dream for us and our world come true. Now that is Good News!

Prayer
God, help me to be a dreamer. Knowing that dreaming takes time, help me to set aside time to rest and dream. Help me to seek you in all my dreams. Help me to trust that you are always at work, incarnating and making real all that we will ever need as we journey through this life towards meeting you in the next. Amen.

Scripture
Take delight in the Lord,
and he will give you the desires of your heart.
(Psalm 37:4)

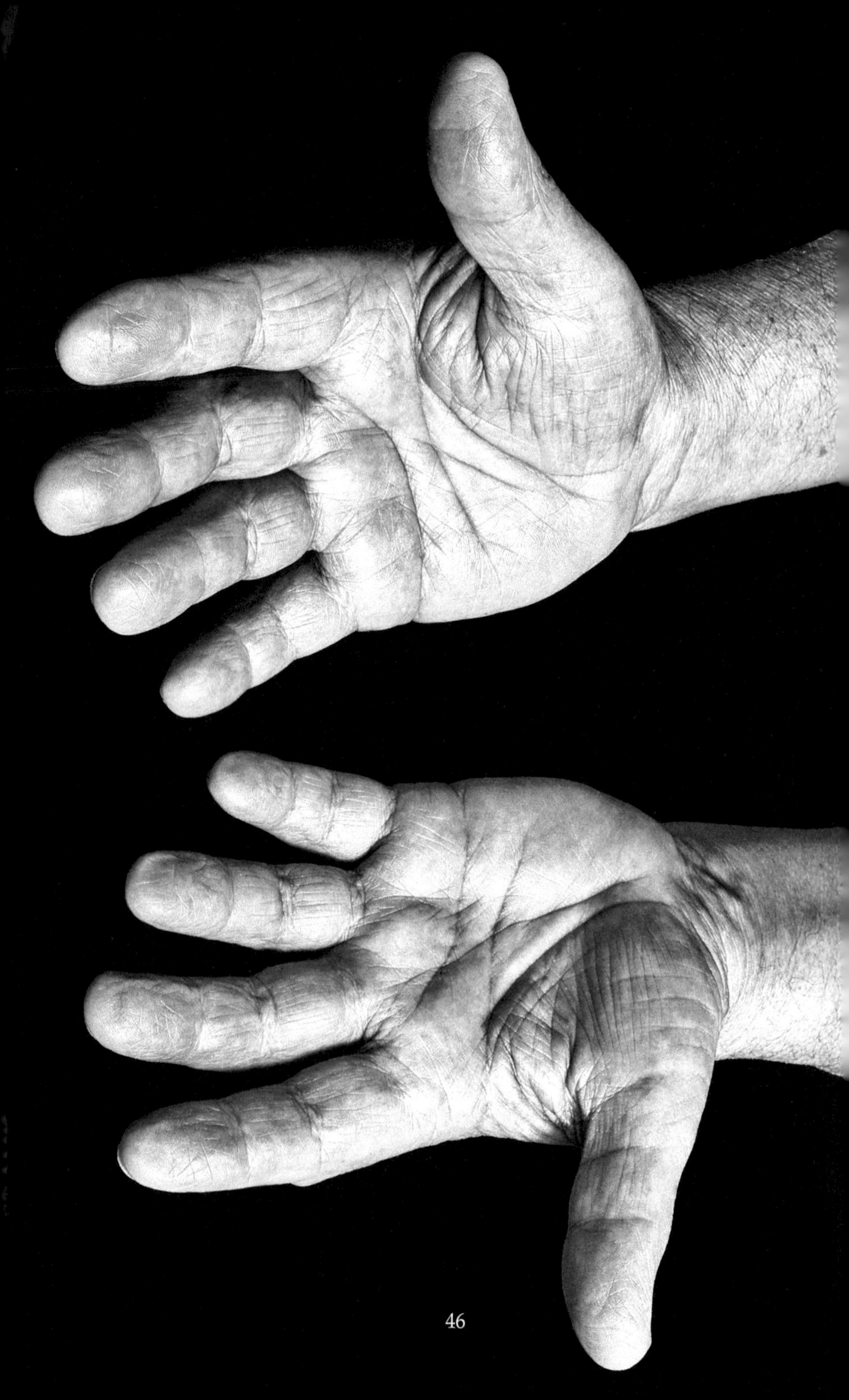

Prayers for commendation

When my priest-friend was very ill and in what would be the last years of his life, he sought to impart to me as much of his wisdom as I could take in. We spent many days and evenings over the autumn and winter of 2012 talking and praying together. He shared memories from his life growing up in pre-Troubles Belfast as well as memories of ministering as a priest at the height of the conflict. He was involved in prison ministry at that time, as well as being caught in the centre of some of the most distressing days of violence seen in the part of Belfast where he lived and ministered, and where I still live to this day. In all these conversations he was steady and wise. He was generous in his sharing and, when it came to speaking about his battle with cancer, he was always so positive and determined to live life to the fullest.

One time I asked him about how he was able to be so positive when also so ill. He told me that each day, when he woke up, he echoed the words of Jesus on the cross, but put his own spin on them. He prayed each day, 'Into your hands, Lord, I commend my cancer.'

Having done that, he went on about his day with as much peace as he could muster. He didn't say these words lightly; he meant them. Nor did he say them blaming God for the troubles he was facing or demanding God remove them. Rather he said them in total trust that God was in them with him and that, in

Prayers for commendation

this knowledge and this divine presence, he would be okay. Tom went to talk to Jesus personally on 11 November 2012. God rest his beautiful soul.

His prayer was not a morose one. It was a hopeful one. It was one that he encouraged me to pray when facing any sort of trouble or worry. He told me it was a prayer that could bring the consolation of the peace of God. Well, my old friend, we are all facing into trouble and worry in the world right now.

Prayer
God, there are so many events in life over which we have no control, and which can cause us worry and anxiety. Be with us in these times and let us know the consolation of your closeness. Into your hands, Lord, we commend our worry and anxiety. Amen.

Scripture
Then Jesus, crying out with a loud voice, said, 'Father, into your hands I commend my spirit.' Having said this, he breathed his last. (Luke 23:46)

It's not about the money

It's not about the money

When I was finishing my time at school and was about to sit my A-levels, our class was given a pep talk and careers advice from a very well-meaning and kind teacher. However the advice, which I've remembered until this day, was possibly the worst advice he could have given. He told us to imagine the career that we'd move into after school, then university. He told us to imagine rising to the top of the profession and then to find out what salary that position would afford. He told us to write that figure down on a piece of card and to place it on the desk where we studied at home. His logic was that, if we were looking for motivation to do well, we should look at this figure and remember the money we were aiming for.

This strategy had a few flaws for me. Firstly, at age seventeen, I had no idea what I wanted to spend the rest of my life doing. I had thought of being a priest. Then I thought of being a teacher, then an actor, then a writer, then a musician, then … I shared my quandary with the teacher. 'Just write down the salary of a dentist. They earn loads', was the reply. 'But I don't want to be a dentist.' 'I know. But write down the salary and keep an eye on the money.'

Keep an eye on the money. And there was a second flaw for me. I'd grown up in a house where there wasn't a lot of money, so appealing to a desire for money, while intriguing, was futile for someone who had no real concept of the figures that top professionals earn. More than this, it seemed a bit distasteful. Even at seventeen, I wanted to shout, 'I'm not all about the money.' Looking back now, I baulk at that advice I was given. It was given with a good heart; I have no doubt. But what did it say to me? What would I say in response now?

Choosing a career or job, or anything else for that matter, on the basis only of what it gives you in material terms is a surefire road to dissatisfaction. My own experience of chasing the money from time to time tells me this also. You can always want more, you see. So, if having lots is your inspiration, you'll always be chasing more and more. Choose a job or career based on multiple factors including salary and job satisfaction, balance between job and family life, making a difference, and you'll have a better time of it.

Having money is not a bad thing. In fact, it can be a very good thing for you, your family, for others in need. But having the acquisition of money be the thing that marks out whether you're successful or not? There are better markers for success. Try love, friendship, being a person of peace, making a difference in the world, finding contentment. If these come along with money, cool! But don't make money our first marker for success.

It's not about the money

Prayer
God, thank you for all the material things we have. Help us to recognise when enough is enough and not be all about material things. Help us to see those around us who do not have enough and to help where we can. Help us to seek satisfaction in relationship with you, with others and with the world around us. Amen.

Scripture:
As for those who in the present age are rich, command them not to be haughty or to set their hopes on the uncertainty of riches but rather on God, who richly provides us with everything for our enjoyment. (1 Timothy 6:17)

Looking deeper: seeing the 'process' behind the 'product'

I sometimes play in a band, covering for full-time members when one is unable to play. I play bass when the bass player isn't available and guitar when one of the guitar players isn't available. The last gig I played was a wedding party, with a hundred or so guests. We came on stage at nine and played until midnight. For the most part we played really well, and the crowd seemed to really enjoy it. Those who came out that night saw a three-hour set of music, and they will have judged our band on that three-hour set. That was the product.

What they didn't see, of course, was the three-and-a-half hours it took us to transport all our stage equipment to the venue, set the gear up, do a sound check, make ourselves presentable and try to look like it was all effortless! That was the process. Now in the entertainment business, it's all about the product and those who engage in it know this. So it is right that our band be judged on the product. And, thank God, the product was pretty good, even if I do say so myself. But most of life is not a matter of entertainment nor is it business. It is real life. It is relationships. It is people walking a path. And often that path is a difficult one, unclear at times, with many twists and turns.

It strikes me that people are quite often judged on the product, that is judged on what we see before us at any given time. Often we see people who are grumpy or angry, or people who are in a real mess or in a state of breakdown or in relationships that are chaotic or problematic. In these cases the product we see isn't very good. And so if we judge on the product alone, we can make judgements like, 'He is a mess', 'He is crazy', 'She is a real pain in the ... '

It would be a temptation here to fall into the trap of judging ourselves as being somehow better than other people.

What we don't see as clearly is the process, that is the life experiences and circumstances that have led the person to where they are. What would we see if we did? Might we see that the person has had a serious struggle? Would we see that the person has been hurt/abused/mistreated along the way? Would we see, perhaps, that the person is doing the best they can with what they have and what they have been given? If we did see this – the process – would we be less judgemental? I know I would.

It may be that it is much more fruitful for us all to simply accompany each other along the path of life, always holding on to what is good and wholesome in each other and hoping to bring out the best in each other. That would make for building communities of real love. And that is a product I would love to see!

Prayer
God, help me to be less judgemental of people. Help me to see behind what seems to be obvious and see the struggle, courage, and dignity in everyone I meet. Help me in life to concentrate on the process of living well, rather than to obsess on needing to produce great results all the time. Amen.

Scripture
Bear one another's burdens, and in this way you will fulfil the law of Christ. (Galatians 6:2)

56

Stripping back

Some years ago, my parents decided to get the walls of their living room papered. They realised that they had allowed one layer of wallpaper to be stuck on top of another for years now. They would need quite a bit of help to strip the paper back this time, so that the new paper could stick well to the wall. They engaged my brothers and I to do the job.

We set about stripping the walls of our parents' living room. The first and most recent layer of paper came off quite easily to reveal a layer of paper a few years old. We remarked that we had forgotten that paper existed until we saw it revealed.

Taking that layer of paper off we revealed another layer from few years before that one. The same happened as we stripped that layer off; it revealed another layer. And so the process went on. An interesting thing began to happen. We began to remember the wallpaper better the further we went 'back in time'. Our conversation became more animated as well. We began to laugh at the colour and pattern of some of the layers. We found that a particular wallpaper reminded us of our childhood. It reminded us of friends and relatives from then as well and events both happy and sad. It allowed us to talk and laugh in a way that felt really healthy.

We removed the last layer and got to the plaster. It was cold and grey, and patchy and cracked in places. The room sounded echoey and bigger. There was no more wallpaper to soak up the sound. We had gone

Stripping back

right back to a time long forgotten. And there in the plaster, written in pencil, were little messages and pictures we had drawn as children, stick figures and names.

A date (from the 1970s) stood alone on one part of the wall, written by my father. There were measurements in feet and inches he had used to calculate the paper needed for the first layer of paper on this wall of what would have been at that time, his and my mother's new house. A new house to bring up their family in love and in faith and in hope. And so they did. And with the passing years they papered the walls with new paper and papered our lives with new memories.

In the moment staring at the plaster, I felt brand new again. I felt reconnected to a past era. I realised I had stripped back not only wallpaper but also layers of the story of my life. And when I stripped it all back, there was simplicity and love. Oh to dwell in the truth that is simplicity and love!

Prayer
God, grant us the time and the ability to strip away all layers of worry, anger, lack of forgiveness and grumpiness that prevent us from connecting to the reality of our lives.
Help us to process the memories of our lives – good and bad. Help us to be grateful for the people who came before us – our parents, grandparents and those who cared for us as we grew up. Amen.

Scripture
So if anyone is in Christ, there is a new creation: everything old has passed away; look, new things have come into being! (2 Cor 5:17)

3
Sailing Home

61

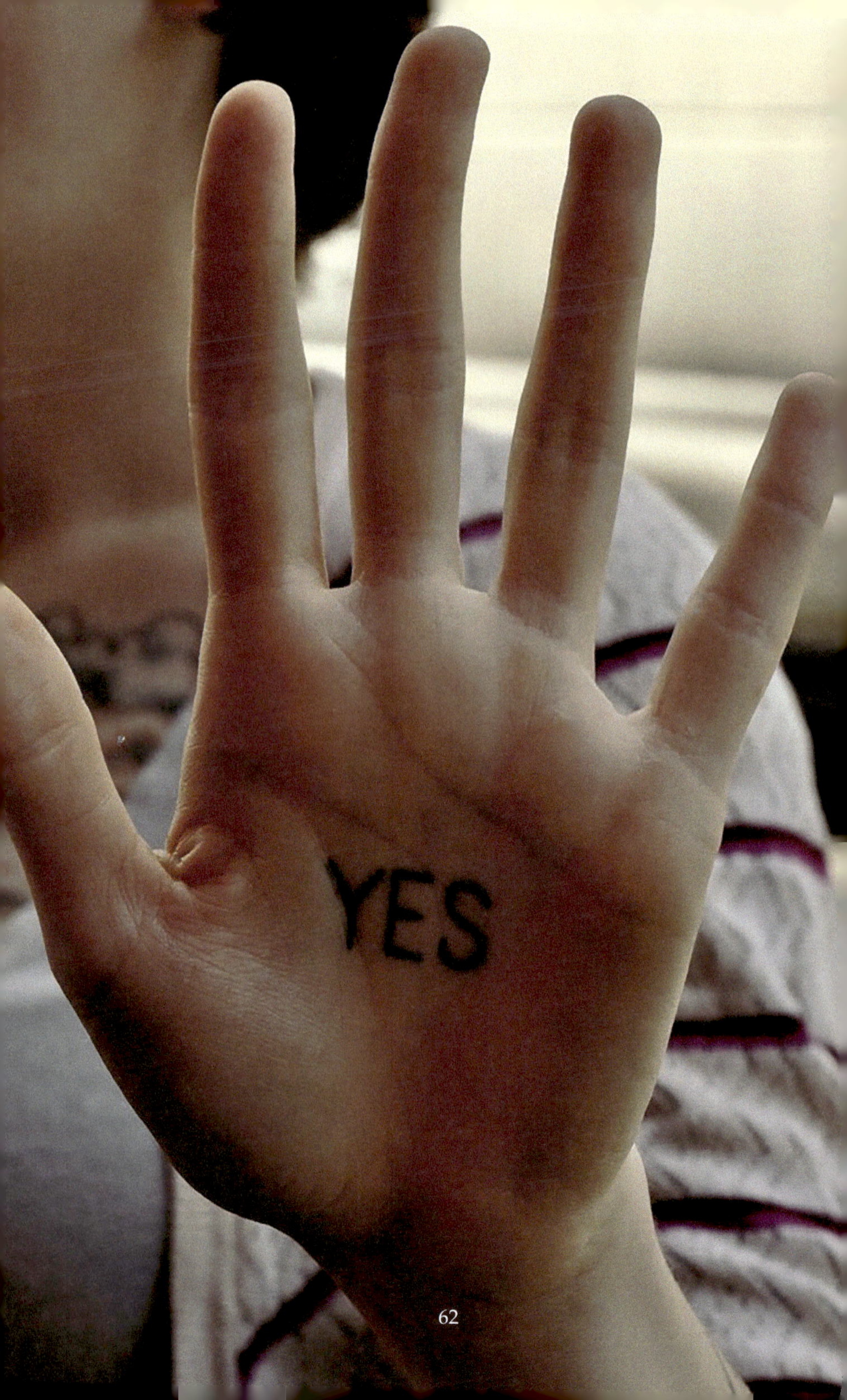
YES

The importance of saying yes

About thirty years ago Yoko Ono had an art exhibition here in Belfast. My memory is that it was quite an eclectic mix of art pieces and media. I was particularly caught by one of her pieces. It consisted of a stepladder with a piece of paper hanging from a piece of string attached to the ceiling above it. It was a small piece of paper and only when you climbed the ladder could you read what it said. I climbed up steadily and strained to read it. On the paper was one word, 'YES'. I climbed down the ladder with a smile on my face. I wonder if that was part of Yoko's plan for those who looked at this piece of art?

Saying 'Yes' is a powerful thing. Think now of the people in your life who have said 'Yes' to you: 'Yes' to supporting you, 'Yes' to helping you out, 'Yes' to rescuing you from some difficult situation, 'Yes' to your vocation or life partner, 'Yes' to offering loyal friendship.

Saying 'Yes' is not always easy. It's often easier to approach life from a 'No' perspective. Indeed at the art exhibition visited that day, someone who was none too impressed had written in the comment book sitting at the door, 'Yoko, Oh No'. Clever in one way, I guess. But it's so easy to say 'No'. To limit what we experience to 'No', to not want to see any good in the experiences we meet. It's safer, I suppose. It is certainly less risky. It expends less energy. And sometimes it is right, necessary even, to say 'No'.

The importance of saying yes

Yet good often comes from a 'Yes' approach to life, a can-do approach. Part of the growth in wisdom we are invited to develop is knowing how to discern between what should be said 'Yes' to and what should be said 'No' to.

In our Christian tradition we recognise and magnify Mary's 'Yes'. She said 'Yes' to God and her only question was 'How will this be done?' No preconditions, no worries, no bargaining, no self-indulgence. She took a 'Yes' approach to life and what a life it was!

> **Prayer**
> Help us to discern what you ask us to say yes to and what you ask us to say no to. Thank you for those who say yes to a life lived for others much more than for themselves. Help us to emulate them. Amen.
>
> **Scripture**
> Then Mary said, 'Here am I, the servant of the Lord; let it be with me according to your word.' Then the angel departed from her. (Luke 1:38)

A deeper brush

A deeper brush

Each morning I spend about two hours with my dogs before work. We walk together as I do my praying and thinking for the start of the day. I feed them, clear up after them, and then I brush them. Now I've got three dogs and each dog has a different type of coat. Charley's is short and fine. Freddie is just a pup, and his coat at the minute is frizzy. Finally there's Cody. His coat is very long and wavy. He is a cross breed, part St Bernard and part Bernese Mountain Dog. He's big and hairy. As I was brushing his coat this week, the brush I was using got overloaded with hair. It couldn't take any more, and it was becoming ineffective. It struck me that I needed to change brushes. I needed a deeper brush to remove all the excess and dead hair from Cody. And so I picked up a brush with a rigid, fine comb, and it did the job very well indeed. It got deep into Cody's second undercoat.

There are times in all our lives when we need 'a deeper brush', when life delivers us circumstances or experiences that let us know we need to go deeper into ourselves or our understanding of the world to grow. Often it is in the face of crises or even disasters that we come to know this. They are what can 'clog' us up, stop us in our tracks. Perhaps the pandemic and subsequent restrictions was one such event that lets us know that we need to re-evaluate our priorities, change our plans, or maybe even let go of our plans altogether. They might also be times of transgression, when we act in a way that we know goes against what we believe is a good way to be in this world.

A common and understandable reaction to all these types of experiences is for us to lose hope or to become down, angry or even frightened. Understandable, yes. But could we perhaps look at these experiences as being signals that we need to/are able to find a 'deeper brush'? A deeper brush for us may be those practices that allow us to shed excess baggage or those thoughts, feelings and behaviours that hold us back.

Some find the 'deeper brush' in spiritual and religious practices such as prayer, meditation and contemplation. This giving some time each day to feel truly rooted in the love of God will allow us to go deeper and deeper into the meaning of life.

> **Prayer**
> God, life can be so complicated and busy that we fail to remember the importance of taking time to speak with you. Help us to grow in our prayer life, always remembering that you are with us, encouraging us and desiring the best for us.
>
> **Scripture**
> In the morning, while it was still very dark, he got up and went out to a deserted place, and there he prayed. (Mark 1:35)

Not walking on by

It was the kind of day when things seemed to go wrong. It was around lunch time, and I was already in a fluster. I was in Belfast city centre rushing from one appointment to another with way too much on my mind. As I walked through the city crowds a man in his forties approached me and said, 'Excuse me, could you help me out? I've no bus fare to get to Banbridge.'

It barely registered with me that he looked dishevelled and that he had a look of sadness and shame on his face. It barely registered with me that his clothes were old and dirty and that he carried an old, battered rucksack. However I was too caught up in my own 'difficulties'. My answer? Without slowing down at all I said, 'No.'

'No.' That was it. I said 'No' and walked on by. It took fifteen paces for my conscience to break through my ego. I stopped in my tracks. I felt such a wave of guilt, shame and anger at myself. How could I have behaved like that? Not only did I not help this guy out, but I was also rude and dismissive to him. I turned round and looked back to where I had seen the man, but he was gone. I walked back but couldn't see him. I spent about half an hour searching the city centre for him, ten pounds in my hand. But I didn't find him. And if I had, giving him money would have been as much about assuaging my guilt as a genuine desire to help.

This happened almost twenty years ago. And yet, from time to time it comes back into my mind. I guess on some level I shocked myself by behaving in that way. Walking on by is the easy option. It allows us not to see or not to have to be with the poor, the hurt, the vulnerable. It allows us to keep ourselves wrapped up in what is going on for us and us alone.

Not walking on by

And yet, we are presented with such opportunities daily. How often we come across people during our normal routines who are homeless, hungry, injured, worried, sad, lonely. Sometimes we just need to open our eyes a little differently to see them. Mainly it means getting beyond our own needs and worries or fears. And when we can do this, we are able to make such a difference to people when they need it most.

Why don't we all look about ourselves and honestly ask, 'When do I walk on by?' Is it by not helping homeless people? Is it by not supporting good charities? Is it by avoiding the sick or the lonely? Who are the people in my life calling for attention? Whatever it is, it is never too late to stop walking on by.

Prayer
God, we are truly sorry for the times we 'walk on by' and ask for forgiveness.
We ask for strength to atone for the times we 'walk on by', by doing good works and helping those in need around us. For the times that we have been 'walked on by' ourselves, we ask for your comfort and the ability to forgive. For the homeless, the needy, the poor, the displaced, the hurt, the vulnerable, we ask that you send healing, consolation and comfort.

Scripture
Whoever is kind to the poor lends to the Lord, and will be repaid in full. (Proverbs 19:17)

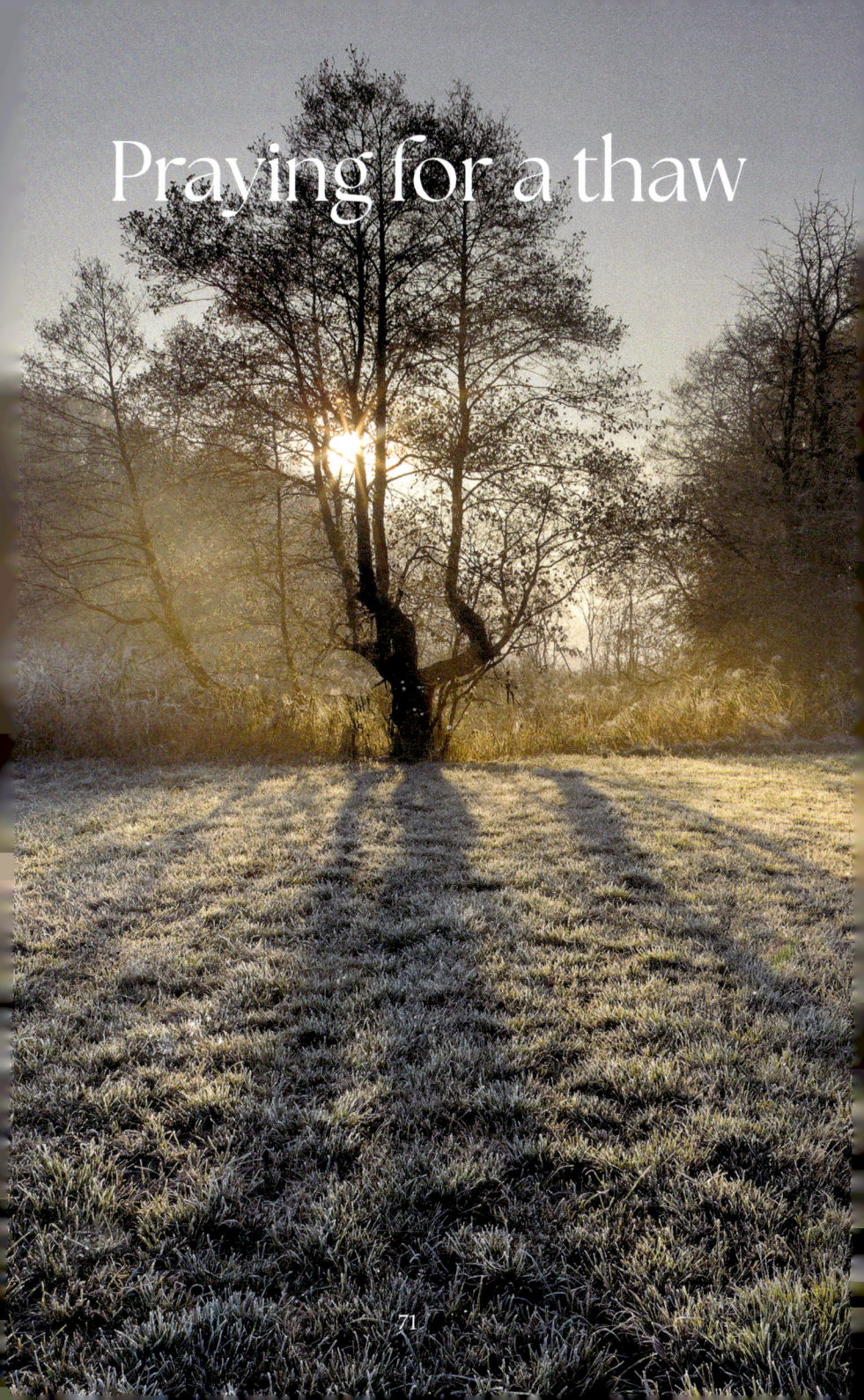

Praying for a thaw

Praying for a thaw

I was out walking my dogs one morning after a big fall of snow. My local park turned into a winter wonderland in springtime! It was glorious. I left the house early, so I was able to walk on virgin snow, my footprints and the paw prints of my three dogs being the only marks in an otherwise smooth, brilliant, white sheet covering large stretches of grassy fields.

As we four wandered through the frozen landscape, I was reminded of Guy Verhofstadt, a Belgian member of the European Parliament, who said of the land I live in – Northern Ireland – that we are stuck in a 'frozen conflict', a not-quite-over-conflict. It was a profound and, sadly, a profoundly true comment. It stayed with me as I walked.

Some minutes later, I found myself at a part of the park where I was flanked by a wall on one side and a neat line of trees on the other. As I walked the path between the two, it started to rain … or so I thought. Big drops of water hit my head and head the ground all around me. I was a bit perplexed, because it was one of those crisp, dry mornings and there was still frozen snow all around me on the ground. I stopped and looked up to see from where these drops of rain were coming.

A second or two later, I realised that it was not raining at all. Rather a thaw had begun, and the first to thaw were the snowflakes and icicles on the branches of the trees. There's a thaw coming, I said to myself.

Suddenly I was overwhelmed with emotion. I felt deep in my heart the need that so many people have to experience a thaw in their lives. In terms of politics in Northern Ireland, we need a thaw in our relationships with each other. We need a thaw in the hearts of those who are consumed with division and violence. This is the thaw that we need if we are to move on from the 'frozen conflict' that Guy Verhofstadt talked about.

My mind went on to think about how, aside from political matters, many of us need to experience a thaw in our lives. As I stood there, a prayer rose from within me.

Prayer
God, thaw the frozen heart that holds hatred, division and violence to be the way forward. Thaw the heart frozen by grief and all to experience consolation and peace of mind. Thaw the heart in need of healing from hurts, old and new. Thaw the hearts of all of us that we may see the good in each other and the woundedness we all carry. Send the heat of your love to all in need of that. Amen.

Scripture
A new heart I will give you, and a new spirit I will put within you; and I will remove from your body the heart of stone and give you a heart of flesh. (Ezekiel 36:26)

Small steps on the spiritual journey home

My dog Charley is a real firecracker of a dog. He loves rough and tumble with other dogs and playing tug with us humans. Of all his interests, though, chasing a ball and bringing it back must be his favourite. I keep the ball in my left pocket, and Charley knows this. When we are out on our walk and find an open space where it is safe to let the dogs off lead, Charley stands at my left-hand side and stares at my pocket, as if using his doggy magic to make me take the ball out. For my part, I seem to succumb to his doggy magic stare and always oblige him. Once I have taken the ball out of my pocket, the game begins!

Over the years of kicking, throwing or batting the ball for Charley to run after and bring back, I have noticed some things. For one, at the start of the game, when Charley has lots of energy, he runs a long way at top speed to catch the ball. As he has gotten older, I find that he has a little less energy. And so, after a while, as the ball flies w..

......ay into the distance, Charley seems to lose heart a bit, and, instead of running a top speed, he trots to the ball. When this happens, rather than dipping down to grab the ball with the gusto he would have had earlier in the game, he slows right up and lifts the ball almost half-heartedly before trotting back to me to repeat the process. He still has a love for the game, but it seems somewhat dulled.

What I have also noticed, however, is that if I shorten my throw, Charley seems to magically regain his energy, his enthusiasm, his youthfulness even. All I have to do to help him achieve all of this is to hit the ball less far away from him. Simple. And

Small steps on the spiritual journey home

such wisdom for us all is contained in this lesson that Charley has taught me.

In the spiritual life, perhaps in all facets of life, goals that are very far away might be OK when we are young and/or when we have lots of energy and enthusiasm available to us to put into chasing those goals. Indeed we might be able to chase those kind of goals way into old age. But at some stage we will lose energy and far-off goals, once a motivator for us, may become a drudge to follow or worse, may become demoralising for us, no matter how much we love the spiritual life. We need achievable goals – still a way off and still in need of a chase but somewhat still in sight – because they are more likely to keep us energised. Small steps, well taken, might just be the best way to walk home on the spiritual path.

Prayer
God, help us to be realistic in our lives and to treat ourselves and others with compassion and understanding. Let us live as pilgrims, taking one step at a time and trusting that you look after the bigger picture. Amen.

Scripture
In all your ways acknowledge him,
and he will make straight your paths. (Proverbs 3:6)

Getting a tune up

Getting a tune up

Some time ago, while on a holiday weekend in London, I took a walk in the early morning as the city woke up. After a short while, I set out to go to one of my favourite churches in London, St Martin in the Fields. It is an Anglican church just off Trafalgar Square and over the last years it has offered me a quiet, prayerful space to come to begin my holiday. That morning as I entered the church, I realised that it was not going to be such a quiet experience. At the front of the church there was a big grand piano. Sitting or rather, kneeling at it was a piano tuner. He was at his work, repeatedly striking one note and making miniscule changes in its pitch by ... well, I'm not sure how he worked his magic!

I took my seat and closed my eyes, and I tried to pray. But the notes, the notes kept coming. I found it hard to ignore them in favour of my prayers. After a while, I found that I let myself get caught up in the notes and in the changes in pitch that I could just about make out. The sharp notes came down in pitch. The flat ones went up. It became a way for me to pray.

In that prayer it struck me that there are many ways that we can be a bit out of tune in our lives. There are areas that are flat, where we experience a sense of being down, sad, low or lacking in energy. There are also areas of our lives where we are sharp, with ourselves and with others too. In this way, we can be out of tune with ourselves and with others. We can need tuning up so that we can live harmoniously with ourselves, with others and with God's plan for us.

God, through prayer, wants to connect with us. God wants to tune us up, gently, honestly and lovingly. If we are open to this tuning up, we will live our lives as a song written by God and sung beautifully by us.

Prayer
God, allow my mind and heart to wander over my life as it is these days. Help me to notice the flat points. God, I ask you to give me what I need to raise these flat points. I pray for energy, compassion, love. Help me to notice the sharp points. God, I ask you to be my tuner and to help me to take the sharpness out of me. I pray for patience, the ability to forgive and empathy. Amen.

Scripture
… be filled with the Spirit, as you sing psalms and hymns and spiritual songs among yourselves, singing and making melody to the Lord in your hearts … (Ephesians 5:18–19)

4
Arriving in Port

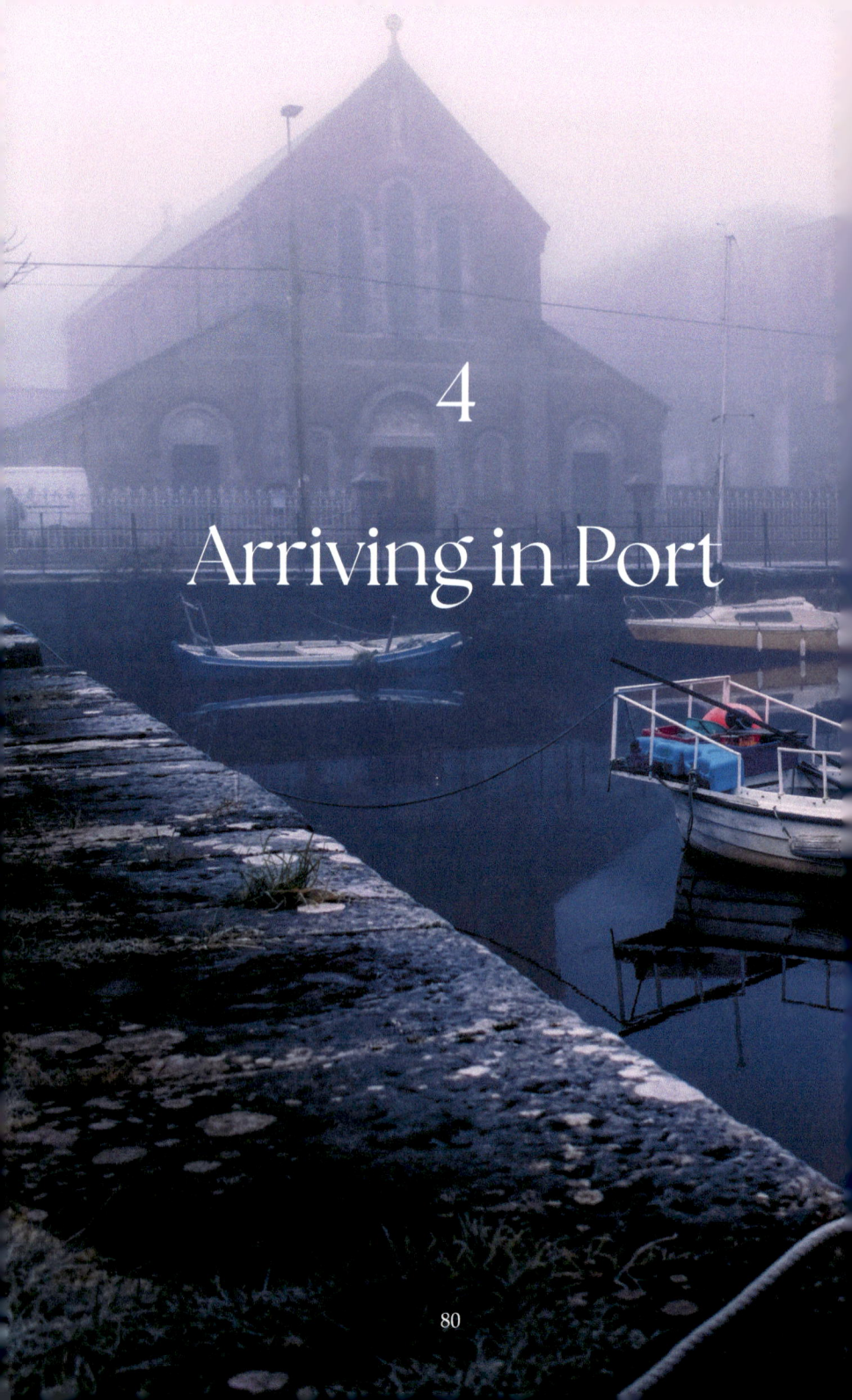

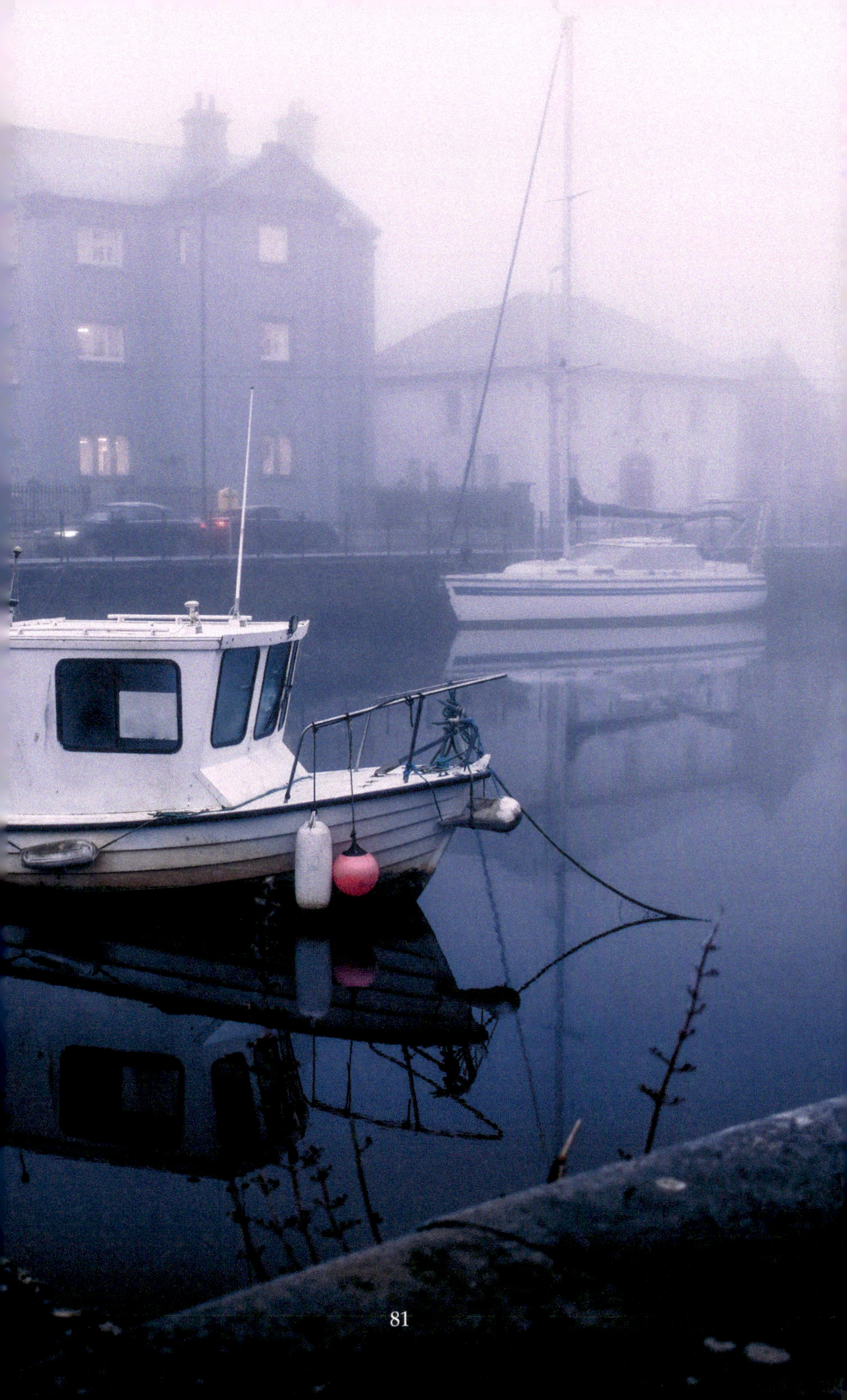

A plan greater than our own

When we are young, many of us make plans for our lives and then set about making those plans come true. We do so with a kind of abandon that feels like freedom. We go where we want to go and do what helps us achieve our plans.

These plans are often good plans. I marvel at the good works done in this world by young people. But sometimes these plans made when we're young are not so good. We know this only when we're a little older and those plans don't come to fruition or do come to fruition but lead to a bad place/no place at all.

This happens to many of us. Through life we make all sorts of plans that don't work out. When they don't, we can become angry, disillusioned and self-blaming: 'All my plans fail', 'I am a failure.' Perhaps there is a greater plan at work, a plan more expansive than our own, a plan in which we play a part but a plan that does not necessarily revolve only around the part we play. Our lives often involve plans with many players, just as important as we are.

Realising this is only really possible by having the plans we make fail. That's a conundrum, isn't it?! Yet I sense it to be true. Counter-intuitive as it seems, the failure of plans is about growth, learning and winning! When this happens, we can know only one thing: the plan was not meant to be; it was the wrong one for the time we were in. The good news is twofold. Firstly the right plan is still out there. Secondly we can discover it and play our part.

How can we do this? Through prayer and reflection. Through discernment and listening for the whisper

A plan greater than our own

(or shout) of God's presence in the plan in front of us. Through checking that we are seeking to be bit players in the plan, rather than stars. And learning from the pattern in the plans that have failed before and moving in different ways.

I believe we are led in life. I know the path can seem so awful at times that we convince ourselves that there can't be a plan. But that's not the case. We are led and loved along the way of a plan greater than any we could make. Anyone, Christian or otherwise, could read the Bible and reflect on the many instances, from Exodus to Luke, of how God has a bigger plan and leads us in spite of ourselves.

Prayer
God, help us to plan wisely in our lives. Help us to seek the good in all we plan for. Help us to keep the wellbeing of others always in our plans. Help us to see failing plans as opportunities for growth. And may we experience love, mercy and compassion along the path. Amen.

Scripture
For surely I know the plans I have for you, says the Lord, plans for your welfare and not for harm, to give you a future with hope. (Jeremiah 29:11)

Praying with your body

Praying with your body

Tiredness, low mood, frustration, despair. These are things that visit all our lives at times. And at times like these, prayer is hard, isn't it? The temptation can be to lose hope and to avoid prayer. However it is precisely at the times when prayer seems hard, that prayer is the very thing we need to attend to. There's a certain irony here, that it is especially hard to pray in these times.

When there are no words that we can pray, sometimes we can use our bodies to pray. This has the advantage of expressing our desire for God physically, even when we don't feel like it. It involves making four body movements or positions. Each one has a meaning and each one becomes a gateway to prayer.

> Position 1:
> Arms outstretched, hand reaching upwards and beyond yourself. This position says, 'I AM MADE BY GOD.' You didn't make yourself. Your parents had a hand in it, but even they did not make you. You were made by God.
>
> Position 2:
> Arms folded, hands touching your chest at your heart. This position says, 'I AM LOVED BY GOD.' Imagine the Sacred Heart of Jesus burning with nothing but love for you.

Position 3:
Arms pushed back behind you, hands open and facing away from you. This position says, 'I AM FORGIVEN BY GOD.' Let it go. Let go all that holds you back from being the best version of yourself. Step into God's wonderful forgiveness.

Position 4:
Arms out in front of you, hands open, palms up. This position says, 'I AM HELD IN GOD'S LOVING HANDS.' Look at your outstretched hands and see that this is how you might hold a new-born baby. This is exactly the way God holds you, like a precious new-born baby.

Hold each of these positions for a few seconds and feel those words and the body positions become one. Allow your hands to fall by your side now. Pause for a while and run through them again a few times, saying to yourself what each position means.

Now let your hands fall by your side again. Pause for a moment and then make the body position that meant the most to you when you made it. Hold that position for a while and begin a conversation with yourself and God. It could begin, 'God, I am making this body position because … ' Stay with that conversation for a few minutes and say what you say and hear what you hear in return. Feel no pressure.

Praying with your body

After a while, let your hands fall to your side again, take a deep breath and end this time of body prayer. I hope you find this helpful in the times when prayer is hard or any time at all.

Prayer
God, help us in the difficult times to keep our contact with you. As St Teresa of Avila said, 'Prayer is nothing more than being on friendship terms with God.' Amen.

Scripture
Now you are the body of Christ and individually members of it. (1 Corinthians 12:27)

Praying for peace

Praying for peace

I remember sitting with a dear friend in the hospice here in Belfast as he neared the end of his life. We both knew he didn't have long left, and he also knew that every second we had together was sacred space. (Oh that we would live our lives together like this all the time and not wait for impending death to focus our minds.) The quality of our conversations changed in those final days. He spoke more. I listened more. He reached deep inside his life's experience to pass on to me the wisdom he had cultivated in his seven decades and more. Some of the advice he passed on in those final days stays with me to this day. God rest his beautiful soul.

Jesus, in his last days on earth, also passed on wisdom. His words towards the end of the Gospel of John seem to take on an intensity that would indicate that he was encapsulating his whole mission into the last conversations he had with his followers before he was taken to the cross. I am always drawn to what is, for me, his starting point in this last passing on of wisdom in John 13:34. After telling his followers that he will not be with them for much longer, he says, 'I give you a new commandment, that you love one another. Just as I have loved you, you also should love one another.'

He goes on to tell them, time and again, that he is 'in' his Father, and his Father is 'in' him, and they both are 'in' us. This signals a mystical and at the same time very real oneness of all creation.

These words of Jesus call us to unity and to peace among all people. And yet war, division, injustice, poverty and climate crisis are still crosses that crucify the world to this day.

We are called to peace. The lack of peace brings us conflict, worry and division. When we find it, though, we find possibility of newness, unity, consolation and progress.

Prayer
God, bring us peace in our hearts and homes, that we may know consolation and seek to bring it to other troubled hearts. Bring us peace in our society, that we may spread cohesion and unity in the face of division. May we walk a path of peace together. Amen.

Scripture
… that they may all be one. As you, Father, are in me and I am in you, may they also be in us … (John 17:21)

Being thankful

Most of us grew up being told that it is good to say thank you. We were told to say, 'Thank you', when we were given something. The other side of that is that we were often scolded if we didn't say it: 'Don't be so ungrateful', or 'Did you forget to say something?' So what happens is that we can grow up feeling that being thankful is simply a duty or a chore. It can become a ritual, just something we say. We almost throw the words out, 'Thank you', without really thinking about them. We lose the power of being thankful. So here's a daily exercise you can do to get back in touch with being thankful.

You could try this today, whether you're at home or in the car or a bus or a taxi. Take a moment and call something to your mind that you are really thankful for. It could be a person or a thing or a situation or even the wonderful world of nature around us. Don't let yourself off the hook here. Really search for something. Then tell yourself three reasons why you are thankful for this.

When you've done that, just sit and be thankful. Really allow yourself to experience thankfulness. Allow your heart to swell with thankfulness, feel the emotion seep through your body. This is worth practicing. Thankfulness is like a muscle that when you exercise it, it becomes stronger. An old friend of mine used to call this the attitude of gratitude. It brings us a sense of calm and a sense of being loved.

When you have called something to mind you are thankful for and have allowed yourself to really savour the experience of being thankful, you could call to mind one thing you could do today to make

Being thankful

someone else feel loved and feel thankful. You could pay it forward. Why not think right now of one thing you could say or do that would leave another person with great gratitude.

A grateful person will want to pass it on to another and so on. And, all of a sudden, we are surrounded by people who are grateful people and who want to pay on their gratitude on being good to others around them. Research has shown that grateful people are mature, inspiring, positive in their thoughts and behaviours, have an appreciation of what they have and are more open minded. That shows that gratitude will be a powerful force for good in our world.

Prayer
God, help us to experience gratitude, even in the midst of difficulty. Help us to practice the two parts of gratitude – feeling it and passing it on – so that we will participate in your plan to build the kingdom and change the world.

Scripture
And whatever you do, in word or deed, do everything in the name of the Lord Jesus, giving thanks to God the Father through him. (Colossians 3:17)

Your heart is where your treasure is

Your heart is where your treasure is

When I was a boy of about ten years old, my uncle gave me a gift. It was a bag of old coins that he had himself been given years before by a friend. My uncle had not looked at them for a long time and knew that I had an interest in history, so he asked if I might like to have them. I remember opening the bag and seeing a dozen or so coins tumble out. They all looked unfamiliar to me. They weren't the size or the shape of the money we were using back then.

As I sifted through the coins, one jumped out to me as being different than the rest. It was a small, thick, brown coin with very rough edges. I lifted it up, and it was heavy. I took it to my dad and showed him. Neither of us knew what it was, but both of us knew it was worth finding out. My dad told me that we should take it to the Ulster Museum for an expert to look at it.

We did this and an expert did look at the coin for us. What we found out was that it was a Roman token coin from at least 1,500 years ago. Wow! I had found treasure. My dad had another conversation with the expert about the value of such a coin and was told it was not very valuable at all. But all I could hear was '1,500-year-old Roman coin'. I felt like the luckiest boy in Belfast. For many years I treasured the coin – my treasure indeed. I collected coins for many years after that, sticking them into old photo albums with descriptions of them below. It was a great hobby to have, but there was only one coin that I really loved

– my Roman coin.

Years went on and the wee boy I was became a young man, and then I got married and moved out of my parent's house and into my own house with my wife. Life delivered joys and challenges and in amongst all of them, I forgot about my old coin … The years of not thinking or to be honest caring about the coin had allowed it somehow to slip between the cracks. Please God, I will find it someday.

Jesus said that where your treasure is, there also will be your heart. In other words, the things we truly treasure captivate us entirely. We get caught up in them and keep them close. My coin appeared to me as treasure when I first found it, but over time I allowed my heart to stray from it in favour of so many other things in life – not all good, not all bad. It got me to thinking about the things I really treasure in life today, what do I prioritise and what is false treasure?

> **Prayer**
> God, help me to see the true treasure in my life – those people and situations that make my heart sing. Help me to give you thanks for this true treasure. Help me to look again at my life and to cut away from it those things that might have appeared at first as treasure but which I now know to be false, a waste of my time or detrimental to me and others. Help me to refocus my time on the things that really matter. Help me to help others, so that their life may be a more treasured experience. Amen.
>
> **Scripture**
> For where your treasure is, there your heart will be also. (Matthew 6:21)

Stopping to smell the roses

After a recent family holiday, I remember feeling the 'holiday blues' when faced with re-entry into the run-of-the-mill, normal routine. One day I spoke to a friend and said that rather than sitting in rainy Belfast I would rather be back in the golden sunshine of the Algarve with my siblings and families all around me. My friend, sensing my melancholy, said some words to me that really struck home. 'I never let good holidays get too far away from me.'

Without going on to explain any further, I knew exactly what he meant; he kept the memory of the joyousness of his holidays and the beauty of the parts of the world he visited alive in his memory. He would sit and remember the holiday in detail and in that way keep the holiday alive inside him. It would never get too far from him. And therefore, he would not experience the melancholy that I was experiencing. Ironically his regular remembering of his holidays allowed him to live much more fully in the present moment than my melancholy would allow me, because I was pining for a time gone by, while he was savouring the fact that it had happened and was grateful for it. He is a wise man indeed!

Maybe my friend is on to something much more fundamental than staving off the holiday blues. I remember a wise old person telling me years ago that it is good to 'stop and smell the roses' and another wise old person telling me to 'put all the special memories in your "Holy Spirit memory bank", so that you can make a withdrawal of a good memory on the difficult days'. We need to see life for the journey that it is. We can see that it is not good to simply rush from one experience to another experience without fully appreciating each day for what it is: a step on the

Stopping to smell the roses

journey that will have afforded us great opportunity for learning and growing.

Ignatius Loyola knew something of this wisdom too. That is why he insisted on his followers learning and practicing the Review of the Day (Examen) prayer, a method of prayerfully processing each day at its end, seeing where God has been active in our lives and where we have either co-operated with or resisted God's good Spirit. We do this so that we might enter into the new day ready to greet it as a friend on the journey of life.

Prayer
God, help us to take time to stop to smell the roses on life's journey. Thank you that we have memories to put into our Holy Spirit memory bank. May these good memories not get too far from us. Amen.

Scripture
Be still, and know that I am God! (Psalm 46:10)

Conclusion

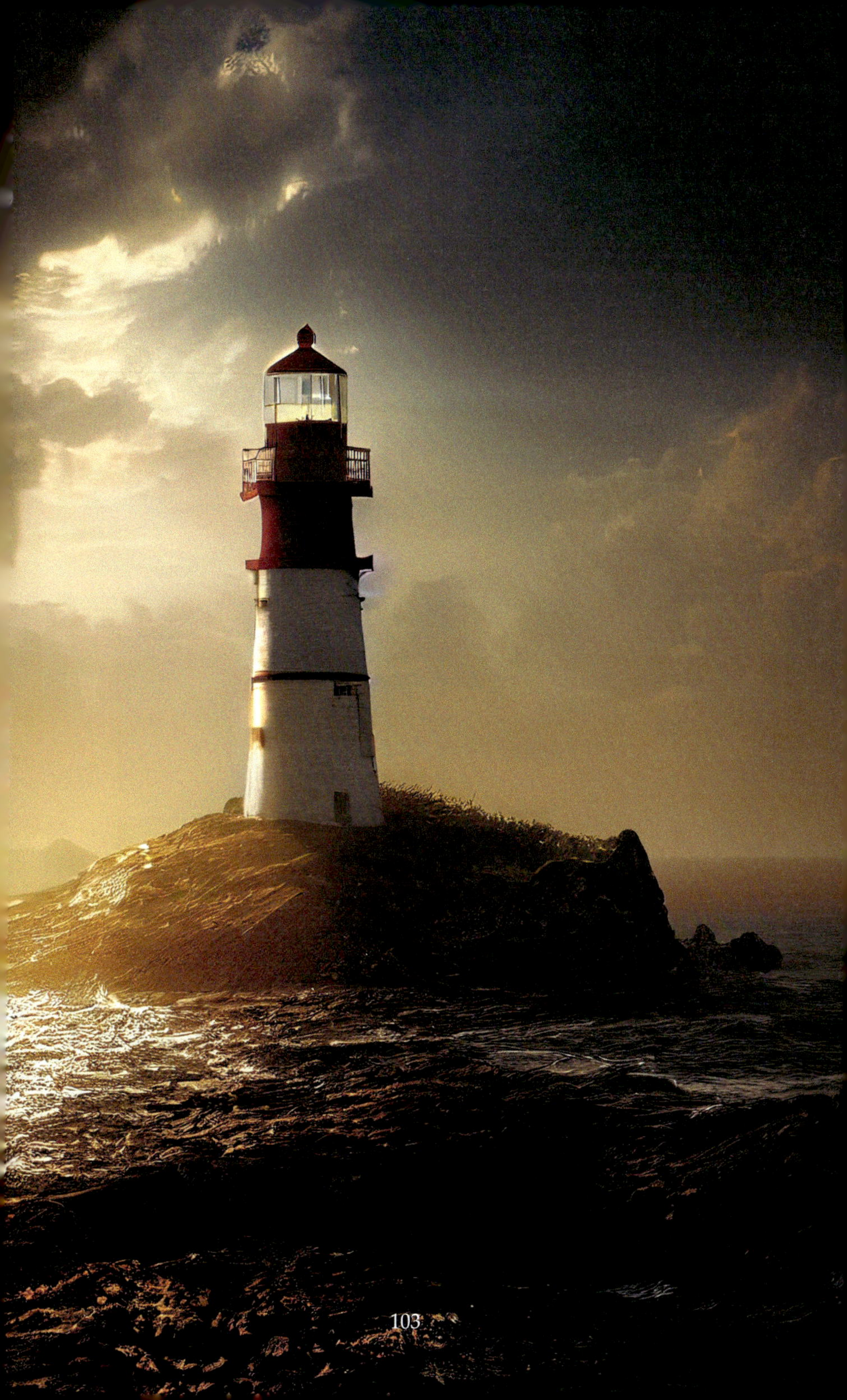

Conclusion

The image on the cover of this book is a lighthouse. A lighthouse shines light out into the darkness, guiding boats to safety. We use it here as a symbol for how we are guided when our lives feel 'all at sea'. At those times, indeed at all times, it is important to remember that God is always with us, shining light to guide and protect us.

Like a captain of a boat in stormy seas longs for the light of a lighthouse, in times of stress, worry or difficulty, Ignatius recommends we keep our eyes on the light, on God. He urges us to take one step at a time and to keep moving steadily on. Life is a pilgrimage where we attend to putting one foot in front of the other, trusting in the God's providence and care. It doesn't mean that all our problems are suddenly solved. Rather we come to understand that there is a way of 'emerging from the mess' that gives us hope and opens up new possibilities. Trusting that God is with us, that there is meaning and purpose in our lives, can help greatly. We still must do our part. We must anchor ourselves lest we get blown about by the winds of chaos. The anchor we speak of here is the anchor of prayer and reflection. We trust that God is with us in these moments and seek to cooperate with God's guidance to reach a safe harbour.

Through the pages of this book, we have tried to reveal the truth that with God's help, we can find a way through, make good decisions and find peace. The miracle, as the stories you have just read hopefully show, is that God is always with us and always trying to reach us, to communicate with us.

Getting perspective, creating space, remembering to pray and not be put off by life's storms is really helpful. The scriptures we have quoted give clues about how others have found God in tough situations and kept hope alive.

Let's keep our hearts fixed on God, face difficulties and problems that arise, and trust that there is always a way through with God's guidance. The lighthouse is always indicating the way home, regardless of how stormy our lives seem.

An anchor in the storms of life

Finding God in the Mess
Meditations for Mindful Living
Brendan McManus SJ and Jim Deeds
136pp €11.95

This best-selling and award-winning book is a collection of meditations, reflective questions and practical suggestions designed for us to find peace and meaning in our busy world, saturated with technology and media.

'... *both a reflective tool for prayer and a map for finding a way through the disarray, confusion and occasional chaos of life*'.
Intercom

God in the nuts and bolts of everyday life

Deeper Into the Mess
Praying Through Tough Times
Brendan McManus SJ and Jim Deeds
120pp €12.95

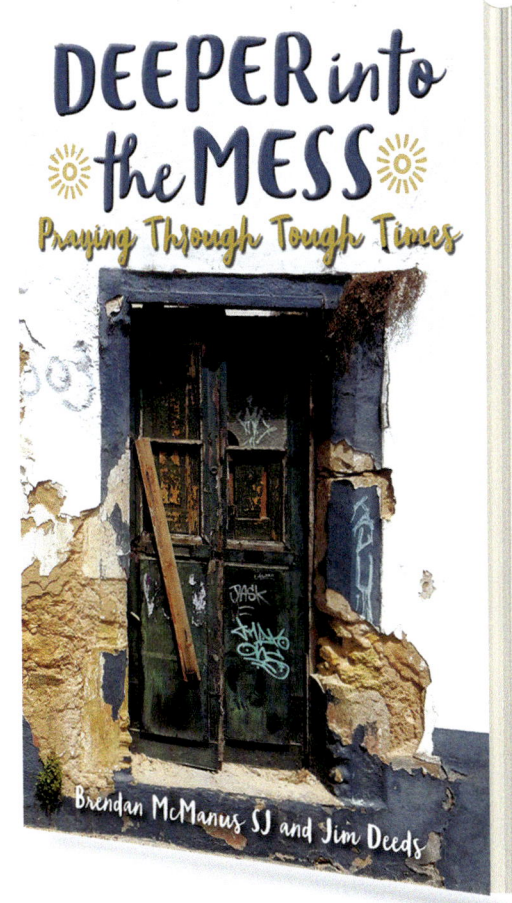

In this eagerly-awaited follow up to the best-selling *Finding God in the Mess*, the authors, in response to requests, address challenging, real life issues such as fear, anxiety, suicide and anger.

'... the authors have established a very popular style of conveying the essentials of Ignatian spirituality'. **Independent Catholic News**